A T M

AN ABRIDGED

TYPING AND COMPUTING MANUAL

FOR

PROFESSIONAL AND CERTIFICATE COURSES

BY

ISSAH Y. WURISHE

ΣΣΣΣΣΣΣΣΣΣΣΣ

AN ABRIDGED TYPING AND COMPUTING MANUAL

ΣΣΣΣΣΣΣΣΣΣΣΣΣ

FOR

ΣΣΣΣΣΣΣΣΣΣΣΣΣΣΣΣΣ

PROFESSIONAL AND CERTIFICATE IN SECRETARIAL COURSES

ΣΣΣΣΣΣΣΣΣΣΣΣΣΣΣΣΣΣΣΣΣΣΣ

WRITTEN BY
ISSAH YAKUBUWURISHE

THE AUTHOR'S PROFILE

I completed HND in secretaryship and management studies in 1998 and Post Graduate Diploma in Organization Development in 2011.

I have since worked in various positions which have enhanced my industrial and professional experience. I have taught typing and shorthand at different school. Now a full time Researcher in Consultancy and also an English Language tutor.

My main objective for writing this book, is to benefit the people with basic and enhanced skills and knowledge in processing information on a manual or electronic typewriter and computer. The relevance of this feat is incalculable, giving that over ninety percent of today's information is processed on manual typewriters, electronic typewriters and word processors.

DEDICATION

For ALL Those Who Love God And Those Who Are Good

**GOODNESS COMES FROM THOSE WHO ARE GOOD,
AND GOES TO THOSE WHO ARE GOOD.**

ACKNOWLEGEMENTS

The adage that man proposes and the Almighty disposes undoubtedly, is the direction of man's fate. In the light of this, it is a priori that I thank the Almighty Allah for this wonderful success.

Secondly, I sincerely thank the publishers GILLBT, for their in valuable service in getting this book published. Most especially, the mangers, typesetters, and every worker there.

I will also want to thank all those who in diverse ways, offered me certain tangible and intangible resources that might have facilitated the success of this project. Among these are my teachers who taught me at the primary, Middle, Secondary, University and Polytechnic respectively.

In addition, my sincere thanks goes to all the good governmental and non-governmental organizations, I have worked with, through which I have gathered enormous knowledge and experience. My experience in research and consultancy empowers me to properly analyse and identify the needs of people. Similarly, those schools I have taught secretarial courses were the very practical centres of this project.

Lastly, but not the least are my family members, especially my late father and mother who supported me so much in my education and wellbeing.

TABLE OF CONTENTS

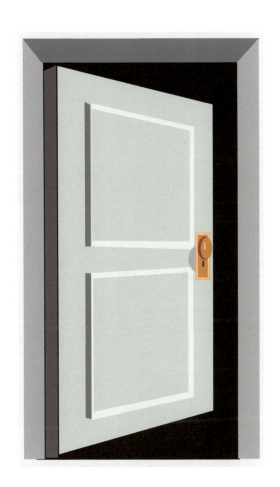

INTRODUCTION

This manual may be assessed by many to be a masterpiece, but not withstanding the fact that none is perfect. The focus group are those who are either undertaking short term courses; such as Typist, Senior Typist Stenographer, Senior Stenographer, and Private Secretary Certificates organized by NVTI, NACVET, and Government Secretarial School; or Long term programmes leading to SSCE, RSA, DBS, HND and Degree. It can also be used by typewriting computer teachers in their lessons.

Undoubtedly, it can be useful to other users, such as working people who desire typing skills to use computers, and portable typewriters.

When you begin using the manual, you gradually notice that, even though it is abridged, but is very comprehensive. Chapter one identifies the various parts of the manual typewriter and explains their uses. The horizontal arrangement of the alphabetic and numeric keys are the same on a computer keyboard, except that, the computer keyboard has additional functional and command keys.

Chapter Two introduces the person to the schooling of typing the keys systematically. Every key on the keyboard is typed with a particular finger, and the systematic typing begins on the Home keys.

Chapter Three is meant to guide the person to becoming a good typist, who can properly display any task. Mastering the keyboard is not enough, until the person is able to follow the basic and enhanced guidelines towards production and applied typing.

Chapter Four is good for both persons learning for the purpose of examination and/or professional progression. Speed and Accuracy are essential tools to good typing. It is necessary that, you type for two to four hours everyday, because every professional secretary needs to achieve and maintain 40 wpm speed limit.

Chapter Five to Ten treats various key subject-documents to be typed at offices and homes. Practical exercises are provided.

Finally, the latter chapters are specifically on computer, about the software and hardware of the system. The treatment here, is a simple dilation of the process of typing on a computer, which is termed computing. Typing and Computing are technically synonymous in application. The basic difference between the two however, is that, whiles as in typing we touch by striking the keys, in computing we touch by pressing the keys.

The primary use of the computer was for work processing and records keeping and maintenance. Therefore, it is very useful to the secretary, administrator and manager. Inevitably, the use of the computer is wide spread today, and for diverse purposes; and any other project which require data entry. Almost all keyboards are horizontally placed and that of computer is no exception, as treated in this book.

CHAPTER ONE

TYPEWRITER PARTS

(1)   **CARRIAGE;** It is the top movable block, that moves from right to left, when you are typing.

(2)   **CARRIAGE RETURN LEVER;** It is a lever attached to the left side of the carriage, which is used to push back the carriage to the right to change to a new typing line.

(3)   **PLATEN KNOBS;** They are knobs attached to the platen on both the left and right sides of the carriage, which are used to roll in and out paper, and can also be used to change to new typing lines.

(4)   **PAPER RELEASE GEARS;** They are positioned on top ends of the carriage and are pulled forward to release the paper from the pager grips, so that the paper can be freely adjusted to accurate position inside the paper guide.

(5)   **PAPER GUIDE;** It is positioned on the top left corner of the carriage, in which the typing paper is inserted through straight.

(6)   **CARRIAGE RELEASE GEARS;** They are on both sides of the carriage, which are depressed to enable the user move the carriage freely from left to right for any purpose.

(7)   **PAPER BAIL AND GRIPS;** The bail is the long metallic scale which is put on the paper to measure the pitch, and hold it against the platen. The grips are rollers around the Paper Bail, which holds the paper firmly against the platen.

(8)   **MARGIN STOPS;** They are movable knobs on the left and right sides of the carriage, used to set the left and right margins on the paper.

(9)   **KEYBOARD;** The Keyboard of many typewriters on the market are the QWERTY KEYBOARD, but the number of keys and characters on them differ from typewriter to the other. All the letters of the alphabets are represented, and all the single digit figures from number 1 to 9 are also represented. Some typewriters, however, do

not have number 1 and 0, and so , they are therefore improvised with, the capital letter I for 1, capital letter O for 0.

(10) SHIFT KEY AND SHIFT LOCK; The Shift Keys are two, located on the left and right extremes of the Keyboard. They are depressed with the first fingers of both hands alternatively, to type initial capitals of words. The left Shift Key is used when you are typing with right hand, and Vice Versa. The Shift Lock is the smaller pair of the Shift Key, which locks in when depressed, to type Main headings, abbreviations, and words or sentences emphasized in capital letters.

(11) MARGIN RELEASE KEY; This key is located on the keyboard, and it is pressed to allow you to complete a word beyond the right margin stops.

(12) TABULATOR KEY; This key is usually marked TAB, and it is used to set column points when typing column or table matter.

(13) SPACE BAR; It is a long bar below the keyboard, and it is the key that is tapped with the thumb to give character spaces in-between words and punctuations.

(14) RIBBON; The Ribbon is the ink of the typewriter, and it is a nylon like thin material, on two spools, against which the keys strikes to make character imprints on the paper.

CHAPTER TWO

MASTERING THE QWERTY KEYBOARD

We learn to type by first locating the position of the keys on the keyboard. The number of keys making up the keyboard varies from one typewriter to the other. Each of the keys has one or two character imprints on it. The keys bearing the letters of the Alphabets bears one character, which can be typed in upper case by depressing the shift key or shift lock.

We begin to type, by first locating and putting our first four fingers of both hands on the HOME KEYS. The Home Keys are. A S D F on which the left first four fingers are positioned, and J K L ; on which the right fingers are positioned

EXERCISE ONE

In this exercise, the student will begin his maiden typing with the Home keys. The first eight fingers of the right and left hands must be suspended on them, to strike the keys sharply. Even when the students master the keyboard, the fingers must be moved forth and back to the home keys. The little finger on the left hand is for letter A, the second finger is for S, the middle finger is for D, and the fourth finger is for F. On the right hand fingers, the little finger is for the; or semi colon, the second finger is for L, the middle finger is for k, and the fourth finger is for J.

a	a	a	a	a	a	a	a	a	a	a		a
s	s	s	s	s	s	s	s	s	s	s	s	s
d	d	d	d	d	d	d	d	d	d		d	d
f	f	f	f	f	f	f	f	f	f	f		f
j	j	j	j	j	j	j	j	j	j	j	j	j
k	k	k	k	k	k	k	k	k	k	k	k	k
l	l	l	l	l	l	l	l	l	l	l	l	l
;	;	;	;	;	;	;	;	;	;	;	;	;

Each of the home keys should be typed five lines each, in order to make the beginners fingers more flexible.

3

EXERCISE TWO

The student will be introduced to the tapping of the space bar, in addition to the home keys. The space bar is tapped with the right and left thumbs or both of them interchangeably.

aaa	aaa	aaa	aaa	aaa	aaa	aaa	aaa	aaa
sss	sss	sss	sss	sss	sss	sss	sss	sss
ddd	ddd	ddd	ddd	ddd	ddd	ddd	ddd	ddd
fff	fff	fff	fff	fff	fff	fff	fff	fff
jjj	jjj	jjj	jjj	jjjj	jjj	jjj	jjj	jjj	jjj	jjj
kkk	kkk	kkk	kkk	kkk	kkk	kkk	kkk	kkk
lll	lll	lll	lll	lll	lll	lll	lll	lll	lll	lll	lll
;;;	;;;	;;;	;;;	;;;	;;;	;;;	;;;	;;;	;;;	;;;	;;;	;;;

Type each line half a page.

EXERCISE THREE

aaa	aaa	sss	sss	ddd	ddd	fff	fff
sss	ddd	aaa	fff	sss	ddd	aaa	fff	fff
fff	fff	ddd	ddd	aaa	aaa	sss	sss	sss
jjj	jjj	kkk	kkk	lll	lll	;;;	;;;	jjj	kkk
kkk	kkk	lll	jjj	kkk	lll	jjj	;;;	kkk	;;
;;;	;;;	lll	lll	kkk	kkk	jjj	jjj	lll	kkk
as	ass	ass	add	as	as	ass	add	add	fass	fad
sad	sad	dad	dad	ask	lass	ask	ask	lass	lad
jass	jad	fak	fak	flask	fall	fall	lad	lad	kad	kak

4

as	a	dad;	ask	a	fall;	lad	falls;	lad	a	kad;	a	dad;
a	jass	fad	kak;	daks	flasks;	add	a	fad	lad;	lass	lad;;
as	a	dad;	add	a	dada;	dads	flasks	fall;	a	fall;

Type this exercise for about five days, to increase your efficiency in typing the home keys.

EXERCISE FOUR

By now, the student is conversant with the home keys, and will psychologically want to try more keys. To satisfy this desire letters G and H, are appropriate, because they makeup the gap to the left and right hands home keys. Type letter G with the fourth finger of the left hand, that is the F finger, and the same finger of the right hand for the letter H.

gag	ggg	hhh	hhh	ghg	ghg	hgh	hgh	fgh	jgh	dhg
fgg	gdg	gsg	agg	jhh	hkh	hlh	;hh	gfh	fjg	fjg
jsh	jha	hkg	hgg	ghh	kgl	sha	fgj	jhf	shl	shl
gas	gas	gag	sag	has	had	hag	lag	lash	hash
hah	dash	dask	fad	lag	gas	gag	sag	had	lash
had;	dash;	ass;	ash;	shall;	hall;	all;	salad;	dalas;
dash;	ash;	shall;	had;	hall;	salas;	dalas;	all;	dash;
shall	add	a	dash	as	had	gas;	had	a	gas	as	a	ash;
as	a	gas	lag;	has	had	gas	lag;	as	a	sag	had	a	lash;	had
a	dask	shall	add	gas	flaks;	gass	flasks	as	had	a	lash;
ask	a	dad	and	lad;	dada	had	a	flask;	salad	had	a	fad;

Continue typing these exercises for about five days.

EXERCISE FIVE

Make attempt to type the top line keys starting with first fingers keys, which are a bit difficult to master, namely letters Q and P . The little finger of the left hand types Q and P is typed with that of the right hand.

| aqq | qsq | qaq | dqq | qfg | qgq | php | pfp | kpp | plp | jpp |
| qass | faq | kaq | haq | fsq | qld | pap | hap | jap | lq; | sqp |

5

gap	fag	pass	paq	sap	pasq	qass	qad	dqf	hgp
gasp	fasp	sap	gap	hall	galp	pass	lap	lag	lag
paq	qad	paq	laq	kaq	gaq	qaq	qah	falq	qalf	saq
kalp;	palq;	qalaq;	slap;	flaqq;	dalp	palq	falq	qalf

Because it is not easy using the small fingers to type, it is better to start them early, usually typing unfamiliar words. Type it for about three days.

EXERCISE SIX

In this exercise, students can begin typing letters W and O. Use the second fingers of both hands, the left for the W and the right for O respectively

www	www	waw	wqw	sqw	ooo	ooo	o;o	opo	lpo
wow	owo	fwh	goh	jsw	kwo	wdl	low	kwo	pow
owo	wow	wao	o;w	swo	low	wdo	okw	fwo	jo
who	wool	low	sold	gold	slow	fold	flow	glow
pod	pod	pool	pok	walk	walks	kows	load	oak
go	walk;	gold	walk;	low	as	slow;	a	pool	of	low	flow;

Type this exercise together with the previous exercise for three days.

EXERCISE SEVEN

You will be introduced to letters E and I. We use the middle fingers of both hands to type them. The left hand middle finger for E, and the right hand middle finger for I.

eee eee iii iii ede ede iki iki fee jii fee jii ege ihi ili i;l hik eie iei

ese eas ged eie eie iei ese ese eas ili i;l hik eie iei ese eas ged eie eie

ease	see	fee	fees	gease	deed	ill	did	kid	did	lid	hip

we	well	oil	pill	leap	sleep	peak	keep	pip	pole	elf

fill	feel	deal	will	gweal	seqast	heal	gill	gallop

We shall feel off a deal; will he go off high pole; we shall; do as he said; his fees will go slow dip; as he said; as a gill; is as a low leap; shall we feel a leap off as he said; do we loaf as a deal off; go slow if is a high load; a fool as led; a leaf falls; go wash; do as a deal; less go off age low; a wolf is like a gale; golf if as good; fall off a hill hope off a road; fail as a we did; let he do;

EXERCISE EIGHT

Letters R, U, T and Y will be typed for the first time. For these characters, we use the fourth fingers of both hands to type them. Letters R and T are typed with the left hand, whilst U and Y are typed with the right hand.

rrr	rrr	uuu	uuu	rff	frr	uhu	juu	drr	rsr	kuu	ulu
aur	rsu	lru	rku	gru	hru	h;r	g;u	asr	lku	ruu	urr
ttt	ttt	yyy	yyy	trt	ftt	yuy	jyy	tgt	dtt	yhy	kyy
ayt	tsy	lty	tky	gty	hty	h;t	g;y	ast	lky	tyy	ytt	tru

try tree trial three through yes yet year yellow yesterday dry dress thurth truth sort whether south southwest east the westeast ridge is situated at the west of the state; yellow sky; plate her hair for the gay party; you are ready for work today; side walk is good for the old and slippery path; do go away;

good sleep refreshes the spirit; will you; shall we; if we go; radio is good for all adults and youth; listen fearfully and speak; thresh thresher; yeast yellow further feather featherless slow; delay delayed helped help; to help her to fall already; yet shall delay so; hello will you fall away to the path; let his heart desire it; without your teleletter to her today; she will go show up here; graduate studies is useful for the elder; astute with hard work; deal fairly with her unless it is too powerful to do;

Type this exercise for about five days.

EXERCISE NINE

For the next two letters, the student should learn to type fastidiously as in the previous exercises. These letters are Z and X, which are typed with only the left hand. The letter Z is typed with the small finger and X by the second finger.

zzz	zzz	xxx	zaz	zaz	xsx	xsx	qaz	zaq	wdx	xdw
sjx	kzl	gxh	zfx	x;o	pwz	xzt	uzy	opz	kyx	tyz
zeal	zero	tax	fax	zetra	uxtra	extra	exart	zepra	zest
gist	golf	loaf	drew	plate	plated	filled	tilled	fill	till

the zebra rattled away with high gear to speed; this year the tax on spare parts will lower or fall; do you fairly sleep at work; at work he sleeps a little extra spare parts are required to repair the lorry low

7

EXERCISE TEN

Read and Type Exercises Ten and Eleven together. They are only five keys, and it is to help you accustom yourself to typing actual words or doing real typing, which involves the combination of many keys.

Students can also type two keys below the home keys now, they are; letter N typed with Fourth finger of the right hand, and letter M, typed with the same finger of the same hand.

nnn   nnn   mmm mmm njn   jnn jmm   mjm knn kmm
nmm mnn flm dkn smn   mln kjn qlm wno pwn nmt
man   main   manly   mainly   mummy   name   namely
same   sunny   lumpy   pump   tommy   yawn   net   netted
annand   anoint   anointed   one   own   wonder   utmost
send tank trunk wanp open gang tank thank thanked namely

the football game was won for the new team in town yesterday; today the man and the woman were really sorry for their deeds; the peak of the issue was when the student presented his story; despite his appeal for adjournment the trial judge still refused him; the desire to transport the people on air was the view of all

please kindly detail your motor rider to the station for a message ; the horse is white at the head and leg with reddish spots on his nose; do not under estimate the followers of the gangsters in the town; the defeat of our foot game team in the game was due to ill fate;

during our wedding yesterday my wife informed me of her intention to remain faithful and loyal to the wedlock; he like playing Tennis game than foot game, volley game donkey ride and tennis; my plans for the party tonight is to make fun, eat and return home early; it is firmly in my plans to deploy all the personnel to the fare; the sense of reading and writing is an essential lesson to learn early; doing good to people is good;

EXERCISE ELEVEN

In this exercise, letters C, V, and B are going to be typed. They form the last batch of alphabets to be typed. We type the letter C with the third finger, it is the finger that types letter D. For the letter V, we use the fourth finger to type it, or the finger that types letter F. It is the same finger that types letter B.

8

ccc	ccc	vvv	vvv	bbb	bbb	dcc	cdc	fvv	vfv	fbb	bfb
cdf	vfg	bfg	bva	sct	jvk	lbc	pbv	ybc	tca	lkv	ghb	slc

ccc   ccc   vvv   vvv   bbb   bbb   dcc   cdc   fvv   vfv   fbb   bfb
cdf   vfg   bfg   bva   sct   jvk   lbc   pbv   ybc   tca   lkv   ghb   slc
vapour   virus   book   bank   come   coil   veil   bail   cool
village   bills   bomb   bill   voyage   curl   country   bring
bought   verge   curve   lincoln   Cambridge   arrival   guide
convenient   conventry   bankrupt   cup   silver   runaway

the boys team won the silver cup after the football match this evening; the girls group was rewarded with a gold medal for being neat; attendance was very poor today in the mosque because of the rain; do not associate yourself with people who are irreligious and uncultured; the car pulled by the roadside; we are expecting the train very soon;

his decision to marry the priestess was happily accepted by all; the chairman of the committee suggested that all the culprits should be freed;; in every society the people of best character are recognised for their example but not for their leadership.

OTHER CHARACTERS ON THE KEYBOARD

CHARACTERS AND THEIR FINGERS

COMMA (,)	Third finger right hand
ONE (1)	First finger left hand
FULLSTOP (.)	Second finger right hand
TWO (2)	Second finger left hand
THREE (3)	Third finger left hand
FOUR (4)	Fourth finger left hand
FIVE (5)	Fourth finger left hand
SIX (6)	Fourth finger right hand
SEVEN (7)	Fourth finger right hand
EIGHT (8)	Third finger right hand
NINE (9)	Second finger right hand
ZERO (0)	First finger right hand

In the absence of zero and one on the keyboard type capital letter O and I.

CHAPTER THREE

TYPING SKILLS FOR PRODUCTION WORK

COMMON TYPOGRAPHICAL ERRORS

1. TYPEOVER: It is when you type a character on an error, as a way of correction, without first erasing the error.
2. ADDITION: When you mistype a word, by increasing or overlapping the characters.
3. OMISSION: When you mistype a word, by leaving out a character.
4. When you type two words together, without giving a character space in-between them.
5. When you do not provide adequate space or no space at all, for the top, bottom, left and right margins respectively.
6. When you give unequal line spacing in a text, without due cause for such display.
7. When a character is not very clear or is blur.
8. Hanging uppercase characters are errors, and they come about when the shift key is not firmly held down, and quickly released just when the key is struck.
9. When typing lines are crooked, because the paper was not properly inserted through the paper guide, and the paper bail and grips are not put on it.

GUIDELINES TO ACCURATE TYPING AND GOOD DISPLAY OF MATERIAL

1. Give six to nine line spaces for the top margin before you begin to type.
2. Strictly follow instructions before you begin to type.
3. Insert the paper straight through the paper guide, and put the paper bail and grips on the paper. This is to ensure that, your typing lines are straight.
4. Give ten to fifteen character spaces for the left margin for elite typewriters, and eight to twelve for pica typewriters. For the right margin leave eight to twelve character spaces for elite typewriters, and six to ten character spaces for pica typewriters.
5. Give one character space in-between words; two character spaces after the colon;; one character space after the comma and semi colon; two character spaces after the full stop, question mark, and an exclamation mark.
6. Leave at least up to four line spaces, for the bottom margin, when you are typing lengthy documents, or multiple page documents..
7. Ensure that your fingers are correctly placed back on the Home Keys all the time after moving them.
8. Type steadily, and strike the keys sharply and firmly.

9. Rarely divide words, and where you do, then divide them suitably: either according to syllable; suffix and prefix; root and derivatives; short or one syllable words are indivisible; and a word cannot be divided from the first two letters, or at the last two letters.

TYPES OF HEADINGS

There are many and varied types of headings, including: the Main Heading; subheading (Paragraph Heading; Shoulder Heading; and Marginal or Side Heading).

1. Main Heading

The main heading of every document should either be centered, blocked, or marginalised depending on preference or specifications. It can be typed in capitals, initial capitals, or spaced capitals. It can also be underscored. In Example 1, 2, and 3 the three different styles of typing the main heading are illustrated.

Example 1: Centered Main Heading

THE LAW OF GRAVITY

The force of gravity was first discovered by Isaac Newton. It is said that, one day the great scientist was sitting under a tree when a leaf or fruit fell on the ground. He then wondered intuitively what force was responsible for such a fall. This initial preponderance and discovery led to the THEORY OF GRAVITY.

Example 2: Blocked Main Heading

THE LAW OF GRAVITY

The Force of Gravity was first discovered by Isaac Newton. It is said that, one day the great scientist was sitting under a tree when a leaf or fruit fell on the ground. He then wondered intuitively what force was responsible for such a fall. This initial preponderance and discovery led to the

THEORY OF GRAVITY.

Example 3: Marginalised Main Heading

When the heading is made-up of two or more lines, all the lines of the heading begin at the same point. It is especially suitable when the subheadings are side headings. An example of a marginal heading display is shown below:

THE LAW OF GRAVITY
A HISTORICAL PERSPECTIVE

The force of Gravity was first discovered by Isaac Newton. It is said that, one day the great scientist was sitting under a tree when a leaf or fruit fell on the ground. He then wondered intuitively what force was responsible for such a fall. This initial discovery and preponderance led to the

SUB-HEADINGS : Subheadings are displayed differently and below are the different types:

1. Paragraph Heading

Paragraph heading is a sub heading, which is typed at the beginning of the left margin and inside the paragraph. Example 4 illustrates a paragraph heading.

Example 4: Paragraph Heading

Wages and Salaries: Wages and Salaries are rewards to workers, after offering a given quantity of service, either measured in time, days, or months.

2. Shoulder Heading

Shoulder Headings are typed hanging above the paragraph. Example 5 illustrates it.

Example 5: Shoulder Heading

Wages and Salaries

Wages and Salaries are rewards to workers, after offering a given quantity of service, either measured in time, days or months.

3. Marginal or Side Heading

Marginal or Side Headings are typed at the left margin, and the paragraph typed on the right half of the page. It is illustrated in Example 6.

Example 6: Marginal or Shoulder Heading

Wages and Salaries: Wages and Salaries are rewards to
                          Workers, after offering a given
                          quantity of service, either measured
                          in time, days or months.

TYPES OF PARAGRAPHS

Paragraphs are very important in material presentation, and therefore their display is equally stylist. There are three types of Paragraph displays, namely: indented paragraph; blocked paragraph; and hanging paragraph.

1. Indented Paragraph

An indented paragraph is typed with the first line of the paragraph beginning four to seven character spaces away from the left margin, and subsequent lines beginning at the left margin. Example 7 illustrates an Indented Paragraph.

Example 7: Indented Paragraph

Division of labour leads to specialization, and most importantly leads to mass production. Specialization seems to be the key to most successes in business and technology over the decades.

2. Blocked Paragraph

Blocked Paragraph is typed with all the lines beginning at the left margin, and what differentiates the paragraphs in the text are the line spacing separating each paragraph from the other. Example 2 illustrates it.

Example 8: Blocked Paragraph

Division of labour leads to specialization, and most importantly leads to mass production. Specialization seems to be the key to most successes in business and technology over the decades.

3. Hanging Paragraph

Hanging Paragraphs are typed with the first line of the paragraph beginning at the left margin, and the subsequent lines beginning two to seven character spaces away from the left margin. Example 3 illustrates Hanging Paragraphs.

Example 3: Hanging Paragraphs

Division of labour leads to specialization, and most importantly
   Leads to mass production. Specialization seems to be the
   Key to most successes in business and technology over the
   Decades.

TYPES OF COMMONLY USED PAPER SIZES FOR
PRODUCTION WORK

1. **A4 PAPER PORTRAIT;** 70 vertical line spaces and 100 horizontal character spaces (Elite), and 70 vertical line spaces and 82 horizontal character spaces (Pica).

2. **A4 LANDSCAPE;** 50 vertical line spaces and 140 horizontal character spaces (Elite), and 50 vertical lines spaces and 110 horizontal character spaces (Pica).

3. **A5 PAPER PORTRAIT;** 50 vertical line spaces and 60 horizontal character spaces (Elite), and 50 vertical line spaces and 42 horizontal character spaces (Pica).

4. **A5 LANDSCAPE;** 35 vertical line spaces and 100 horizontal character spaces (Elite), and 35 vertical line spaces and 82 horizontal character spaces (Pica).

5. **A6 PAPER PORTRAIT;** 35 vertical line spaces and 50 horizontal character spaces (Elite), and 35 vertical line spaces and 41 horizontal character spaces (Pica)

A6 LANDSCAPE; 25 vertical line spaces and 70 horizontal character spaces (Elite), and 25 vertical line spaces and 55 horizontal character spaces (Pica)

CHAPTER FOUR

SPEED AND ACCURACY DEVELOPMENT

Speed and Accuracy are equally important in professional typewriting, therefore, none is sacrificed for the other. A good typist should maintain a steady, rhythmatic and touch typing. Whilst his or her face is affixed on the text, the concentration of the mind is on both the text and the movement of the fingers, in its manipulation of the typewriter.

EXERCISE TWELVE; 200 WORDS TO 5 MINUTES FOR 40 WPM TARGET

Management is both a theoretical and practical activity, involving the science of planning, organizing, staffing, directing, and coordination, communication, controlling, motivation and decision making. These activities are managerial processes which are systematically implemented.

Management systems can be defined as the main structures, poles or pillars upon which an organization is built, and which are apparently necessary for the successful realization of any managerial function. These structures include: Production, marketing, personnel, financial, communication, research and development systems, and any other departmental directory which may be established in an organization.

All organizations according to Howard Barnette 1992, in his book Operations Management, have only five different kinds of resources to work with. These include: equipment, material, money, people and time. The basic idea of resource conversion into usable goods and services involves the adoption of these management systems and the utilization and improvement of managerial functions to achieve the desired returns.

EXERCISE THIRTEEN; 200 WORDS TO 5 MINUTES FOR 40 WPM TARGET

Management Systems in the rice industry in Northern Ghana poses some challenges and acute problems. Food is a basic necessity of life on which man depends on for energy. Rice is a carbohydrate food and is one of the major crops cultivated in the country.

The domestic production level of rice is too low to suffice the enormous population. This has necessitated the importation of rice from abroad.

Nonetheless, rice remains a costly food item for the average Ghanaian. The areas in Ghana where rice is grown include Atebubu, Ejura, Dawhenya, Enchi, Afife, Bolgatanga, Wa, Tamale, Yendi, Adidome, etc. Its cultivation in Northern Ghana is very great and needs much attention and interests of investors.

The rice industry has continually faltered in productivity due to ill-established managerial systems. The industry is dominated by small firms, which are managed haphazardly by their owners themselves. In the first place, most of the firms are not officially registered with Registrar Generals Department and have no office premises and preparations for farming is randomly and poorly planned. Secondly, they are ran by their owners themselves who are illiterates, without the adequate knowledge to apply modern management techniques.

EXERCISE FOURTEEN; 280 WORDS TO 7 MINUTES FOR 40 WPM TARGET

Education forms a bedrock upon which a business can prosper.. Story 1982 writes that Gudgin et al showed that firms established by graduates performed significantly better , in terms of turnover, than otherwise similar firms established by non graduates. Whilst Smith in his study suggests that the nature of education is one factor distinguishing the craftsman type entrepreneur from the opportunist.

On the other hand, the bigger firms have their own peculiar managerial setbacks, such as in marketing, production, research and development, personnel, etc. These managerial systems are not all well organized to achieve the desired goals.

The entrepreneurs in the industry are affected by many setbacks, including lack of machinery and plants, lack of managerial expertise and educational qualification, inaccessibility to capital, unwillingness of farmers to venture into the industry, and the absence of personal wealth.

Thus, for a successful industry, the correct application of managerial expertise and roles are necessary. Management Systems cannot be established and worked on in an environment of peasantry and ignorance. With the enormous potentials of the industry, such as availability of cultivable land, low cost of production, ready market, the application of good managerial systems will certainly raise the productivity of the industry.

EXERCISE FIFTEEN; 400 WORDS TO 10
MINUTES FOR 40 WPM TARGET

Many management theorists and founders have defined the subject in diverse and many ways. Mary Parker Follet defined management as the act of getting things done through people. Henry Fayol, on his part, wrote, to manage is to forecast, and play to organize, to command, to coordinate and to control.

Definitions of management have differed over time relative to the environment under which it is described. Management functions include: planning; coordination; controlling; organizing; motivation; directing; communication; staffing; and forecasting; etc These elements of management are functionally applicable through the management systems. These functions cannot be performed in a vacuum or not through a person or persons heading the system. The managerial functions are channeled through the structures of management. They are; Personnel; Production; Marketing; Finance; Communication; Research and Development; and other departments found to be necessary.

Etienne et al 1992 defined a system as a set of components linked by relatively organized relationships, inorder to fulfil certain functions. Management System uses the middle level management components and linking them together to achieve organizational targets. Without a coordinated process of these departments, no meaningful activity can be performed.

The resources of the business, mainly including: Equipment, material, money, people, and time, are converted into finished goods and or services by the management systems. In an organization, to ensure high performance and efficiency, these management systems are each allotted to line directors or managers. Thus, management becomes a wholesome and functional system only when all the activities of the varied departments are well coordinated and streamlined to achieve the desired goal.

EXERCISE SIXTEEN; 500 WORDS TO 10
MINUTES FOR 50 WPM TARGET

In his book Mastering Marketing, Foster 1982 describes marketing system as the systematic application of entrepreneurship to the almost constantly changing conditions of the present age. It is concerned with the rational and logical use of people, materials, plant, money and other resources to ensure profit, survival and growth over the largest possible period. Marketing system is an entrepreneurial task involving the judicious and speedy disposal of products to the consuming public to obtain profit. An organization customer relationship depends on an effective marketing system. It is the duty of the marketing department to make sure that the goods in stock are sold at approved prices which is profitable to the organization.

The marketing activity is defined in diverse ways. The British Institute of Marketing defined marketing as the management process responsible for identifying, anticipating and satisfying customer requirements profitably. Furthermore, the American Marketing Association defines marketing as the performance of business activities that direct the flow of goods and services from producer to customer or user. The basic marketing techniques include: Production activities; Product management; Marketing management; Sales management; Physical distribution management; etc.

The essential promotional activities for an organization are advertising, sales promotions and public relations. Product management involves managing existing products, product modification, product rationalization, and new product development. Market management is the process of managing existing successful markets, modifying markets, market rationalization, and new market development. Sales management involves planning the general sale operation, recruiting and determining the reward for the sales personnel, selecting suitable administrative methods, devising a suitable monitoring service and information system and making recommendations for new adjustment to be made. Physical Distribution management requires the establishment of stock and sales depots, regular inventories and inventory control, efficient transportation and administration. Other marketing techniques include merchandising, packaging, telephones selling, systems selling and commando marketing activities. The latter tool is necessary in situations where competition is keen.

EXERCISE SEVENTEEN; 350 WORDS TO 7
MINUTES FOR 50 WPM TARGET

The communication activity in an organization is defined by Mardock and Scott 1993 as the provision and passing of information and instructions which enable a company to function efficiently and effectively and employees to be properly informed about developments. Communication in a company, also involves the transmission of information to external channels such as customers and the general public and other relationships, as well as the total administrative processes. Thus, the communication system of an organization embraces Management Information System MIS, Administration and Records Management and or Computer Based Systems.

The importance of good management information system in an organization includes: enhancing control on already existing mutual and cordial relationship between employer and employee; employees contribute more ideas towards organizational goals through dialogue; misunderstandings and conflicts are resolved in developing systems and procedures; it enhances efficiency and leads to success; decision making is facilitated and flexibility created within the organizations operations; brainstorming and teamwork is enhanced by encouraging and organizing open forums, workshops, conferences, seminars, etc.

Likewise, the advantages of administrative practices are enormous. Denyer 1980, specifies the two main functions of an Administrative Manager:: The receipt and retrieval, sorting and analyzing, recording, arranging and transmission of information is carried out efficiently, so as to provide an accurate, comprehensive and upto date information service to senior management; the clerical procedures which is a necessary part of the organizations functions in the process of meeting corporate objectives are carried out systematically with maximum accuracy and speed at minimum cost.

EXERCISE EIGHTEEN; 600 WORDS TO
10 MINUTES FOR 60 WPM TARGET

Management systems theory is applicable in all spheres of human organizations, though relative to the sort of classification and identifications given to it. All economies of the world faces similar basic economic problems, most particularly the issue of scarce resources relative to uses. This is why governments are given the challenges and mandate to oversee and consciously direct their economies to meet the pressing needs of their citizens. In order to achieve these targets, interests and responsibilities are classified and assigned according to their respective systems to be directed through them to achieve national goals. Also, economies are dominated by industries and other businesses which are either monitored or controlled by the government agencies for the sake of efficient tax system or for profit. Individuals who set their own targets and strive to achieve them through systematic means wholly own some of these industries and businesses in other economies. The success of all these economic activities in human societies depends on the mode and application of management systems. The establishment and applications of management system is not a matter of chance but a systematic and judicious classification of management processes and tools.

The problems of all societies and economies arise as a result of scarce resources, namely capital, land, labour, etc. To satisfy human wants. The

19

problem of alternative uses and choice arise because of inadequate resources relative to needs. Therefore, the concept of opportunity cost emphasizes the problem of choice by measuring the cost of obtaining a quantity of one commodity in terms of the quantity of other commodities that could have been obtained instead. The basic economic problems center on six questions faced by all economies. The first of them is, are the-country's resources being fully utilized or are some of them lying idle? Despite the scarcity of resources, yet one of the most disturbing characteristics of free market economies is that such waste sometimes occurs This kind of eventuality is described as involuntary unemployment of resources. The second question is what commodities are being produced and in what quantities? This raises the concern for judicious allocation of scarce resources among alternative uses. The third basic question is by what methods are these commodities produced? This is a matter of production methods employed with consideration to their consequences. Another basic question is about how societies output of goods and services are divided among its members. This raises considerations for equitable distribution of national cake, to evenly raise the living standards of the nation at large. Furthermore, the efficiency of the society's production and distribution system is important. Both dimensions, production and distribution call for efficiency and justice respectively. The last disturbing but not the least basic question is about economic growth that is, is the economy's capacity to produce goods and services growing or declining.

EXERCISE NINETEEN; 630 WORDS TO 9
MINUTES FOR 70 WPM TARGET

The overall management systems methods embodies responsibilities of all the systems on a single person or owner. The sole owner is his own employer, financier, marketing manager and basically everything in one person. This type of management system application can be successful if the owner is hardworking, makes and plans good decisions and judiciously uses available resources to the benefit and expansion of the business. He must keep records and accounts and ensures all the time expenditure is far below his income. Good records and accounts keeping will; enable him to dispose his debt simply, thereby enhancing his reputation among his partners. Since the resources base is small, he will need to plan over a specified period towards expansion, and this will involve sustained savings. The partnership type of business can apply to the Delegated method of management systems. In this method, the partners can employ a few hands, one or two persons, to take charge of some categorized responsibility, such as Administration, which is a subunit of communication system. In this regard, the partners will only delegate their administrative duties to the employee but not with full control to make independent decisions. If need be, to employ a second person, or third, will depend on how large the partnership business is and their capacity to pay salaries and wages.

The Joint Stock Company is larger than any of the former two firms, in terms of both resources and personnel. The management of a Joint Stock Company can be complex in some respect, especially those well known in the advanced countries today. This type of company can apply the structured or delegated methods of management systems depending on the resources and capacity of the business. The basic characteristics of the limited liability company are that, it has shareholders that are the owners of the business. They appoint a Board of Directors, who in turn appoint an executive management team, If the resources and the productivity capacity of the company is much appreciated, then their management systems can be structured. In this case, there will be the need to employ specialized personnel to manage the organizational pillars or departments. The management systems will then be established to maximise productivity and profits for the company.

However, if the resources of the company are not too big as expected, then the Board of Directors can apply the Mixed method of management systems. Some structures will be established and other subunits of some department intermarried into already existing structures by way of delegation. For example, a company has already established Finance and Communication departments, and intends to create a new department of marketing but cannot do that due to lack of resources. Then, it can delegate some of the important subunits of the marketing department to both the Communication and Finance Departments. For instance, sales management can be delegated to the finance department, and that of promotional activities delegated to the communications department. The above analysis can be depicted diagrammatically.

EXERCISE TWENTY; 640 WORDS TO 8 MINUTES FOR 80 WPM TARGET

There are many and varied problems associated with the establishment of management systems in any organization. Each of the management structures has its peculiar problem connected to it. The main problem associated with personnel system is remuneration. Remuneration is an important concern because it is the directors of the organization who determine the wages and salaries of personnel. Good remuneration will be a motivation factor to high productivity, whereas poor remuneration can result in unstable working relationships and productivity. Similarly, the problem connected to the production system is efficiency. Efficiency relates to methods adopted by the production system to achieve its production targets. The production is described as being efficient when the targets are achieved but is inefficient when productivity falls below the target levels. Also, serious external economic depressive tendencies pose a serious problem to management systems, especially in marketing system. Economic analyst are unanimous on the view that market risk cannot be completely avoided because it is directly related to the movement in the economy as a whole.

The main problem confronting the financial system is constraints on scarce resources mobilization and rational utilization of these resources. These constraints are evidenced in both initial and medium term financing of the organization. Furthermore, problems arising from the communication system is when wrong and impracticable overall strategies and policy decisions are devised and implemented. Such a problem is especially difficult to resolve due to delays and waste connected with decisions to retract and institute new strategies and decision. The problem affecting Research and Development System is when inaccurate statistical data is approved for use. This can completely lead to misdirection and misappropriation of scarce resources.

Management systems are important as the economy and industry are to the nation and owners of businesses. Every economy and business must be organized and managed on their correct path and principles, except in peasantry situations, where simple methods are employed. Considering the economy as a whole, a nation will need to adopt management systems in order to convert its scarce resources into utilities. The establishment of these management systems will involve the creation of ministries and or departments and assigning and tasking them with specific duties and functions. These ministries represent the pillars of the economy, working together with coordinated efforts to achieve the same goals. Similarly, industries and other businesses will equally appreciate the significance of management systems in achieving their set targets when they properly adopt them. Even in poverty stricken situations, the home of a peasant farmer needs to be properly managed, and for that matter, basically, if not for financial and logistical constraints, he would have wanted to manage his business on modern managerial standards and requirements.

Therefore, management systems is important in the economy, industry and other businesses because of the solutions it can provide to the numerous and varied problems facing each of them. In the first place, management systems are important in offering good marketing management and planning.

The Board System is the most powerful and highest decision making structure in any organization. Except in business, which is owned by shareholders. The Board System in this case is appointed by the shareholders and they can dissolve it as well. The Board System formulates policies and institutes regulations for the Executive Directors to implement.

The composition of the Board System is determined by the definitive article in the constitution or article of incorporation of the organization. The Board is headed by a Chairman and, of course, unceremonial Deputy Chairman, who deputizes when the Chairman is indisposed. The total membership is determined by the article of incorporation or constitution of the organization.

In a limited liability company, the Managing Director or Executive Director, is a member of the Board. The Board appoints the Managing Director and he is at the same time made a member of the Board of Directors. It is the Board System, which certifies his actions and he is their representative to the rests of the members of the organization. The Board members are mostly owners of the company and sometimes those selected to the Board are those who own bigger shares in the company and are thought to have the capacity to work on behalf of the rests of the shareholders.

A limited liability company also appoints a substantive Company Secretary as provided by the incorporation laws, and he serves as Secretary to the Board System statutorily, and are appointed by the functional shareholders based on their merits.

The Board System ensures the smooth running of the organization through consultation at Board meetings. At the end of Annual General Meeting and other important meetings, the Board issues directives to the Executive Directors to implement.

The implementation of such directives are reviewed at subsequent Board meetings to ensure laudable monitoring and evaluation. The Executive Director and his line managers are the team of implementers. The success of the organization in terms of profit and expansion depends on the good policies and directives of the Board.

At the meetings, decisions relating to labour turnover, expenditure for the year, market exploration and capitalization, business expansion drives, shareholders dividends, matters relating to shares floated at the stock market are some of the paramount issues considered.

The Board determines how much labour force is needed by the company for impending fiscal year. Labour turnover is ascertained by the Personnel System and presented to managing system. The managing system verifies and amends and presents it to the Board System for approval. The Board System ultimately decides the exact personnel to be recruited.

Every organization prepares its annual budget and upon approval by the Board System, becomes the standpoint for any policy decisions. The organizations expenditure for the year will therefore cover cost of management systems and investment capital.

The demand for the company's commodities is very important, hence the need for vigorous markets exploration initiative. Already existing markets should be maintained and sustained, and new market avenues should be explored and penetrated. The Board System will consider marketing proposals presented and approve appropriate and suitable policies.

Business expansion takes several forms. The business can expand by increasing its production levels such as 100 tones to 200 tones. This can be achieved by expanding the production base and the amount of resources used. This entails the purchasing of new plants and machinery and other production accessories. Another way of expanding a business is through diversification. The Board can decide how the company should expand either by related or unrelated diversification or by expanding its production base. Nevertheless, whether a company is expanding by diversification or by expanding its production base, will still require vigorous measures towards market exploration and capitalization, through the means of marketing research and other departmental research. The systems will therefore pursue this goal by resorting to its Research and Development System to undertake the feasibility and research studies.

The Board System also determines the payment of shareholders dividends. This is done only after cost of management systems, including tax, is deducted from gross profit.

EXERCISE TWENTY TWO; 500 WORDS TO
5 MINUTES FOR 100 WPM TARGET

There are scores of big and small industries operating around the world. The size of each industry depends on the type of quality of production of its products. The big industries include the Rice Industry in China, Wheat industry in USA, Timber industry in Brazil, Oil industry in the Middle East, Gold industry in South Africa, etc. The small industries include The Rice industry in Ghana, Palm Oil industry in Malaysia, Fishing industry in Mauritania, etc.

The small industries mentioned above are among many of their types around the world. All of them are managed according to local conditions affecting them. These small industries are most affected by general economic trends on both the local and global markets. Such as fluctuations in prices and new regulations. Despite these hindrances some of them still grow and prosper and has brighter future. Those of them who are successful are those who have put in place management systems that are competent enough to influence trends to their advantage. Most of these industries except a few, are partially controlled by the central government, especially in areas of financing and marketing. Production of the product is done by the people who cannot raise enough capital to produce. The government offers them credit schemes and in turn purchases the products from the people at dictated prices for export. Nevertheless, there are chances for increased productivity if the correct management systems methods are adopted. In otherwords, the farmers themselves can begin to adopt modern management tools and processes to increase their efficiency and productivity on their fields of production and sales. The method of management systems appropriate for such industries will depend on the type of business organization operating in the industry.

A case study approach on Management Systems in the small rice industry in Ghana is that, the rice industry is predominantly private small scale farmers, such as Gushie Farms. Except a number of organizations, which are jointly owned by government and private financial institutions, such as Nasia Rice Company. Then, some bigger organizations solely owned and established by the government, not only to oversee and promote the production of rice, but other food and cash crops, such as Ministry of Food and Agriculture, Irrigation Development Authority, Agricultural Sector Investment Project, Seed Division, Savanna Agricultural Research Institute, etc. The privately owned enterprises are solely directed and managed by their owners.

CHAPTER FIVE

CORRESPONDENCE

In broad terms, correspondence can be described as information exchange between parties. In written correspondence, invariably, there are two main means of correspondence, namely Letters and Memoranda. Secretaries will therefore be dealing and typing these kinds of correspondence in their final examinations, and ultimately at workplaces.

LETTERS

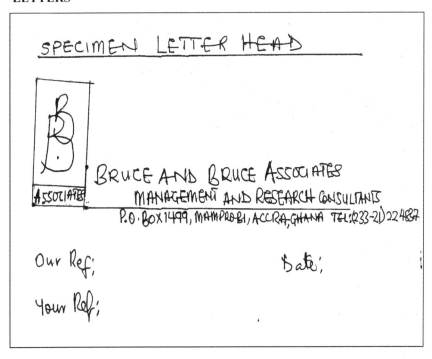

Letters are external communication, which are normally posted or hand delivered. There are various types of letters typed in the offices of both private and public organizations. The different types of letters typed are Formal Personal Letters; Informal Personal Letters; Business Letters; Circular Letters; and Civil Service Letters.

MEMORANDA

Memoranda are internal communication tools. They are normally preformatted as practiced in most well established organizations, or in the absence of forms, ordinary A4 or A5 papers are used to type them They are in various sizes, depending on the length of the information, which determines its paper size. They can also be typed in various styles, either in Blocked or Indented formats.

SPECIMEN MEMORANDUM FORM

Commission on Human Rights and Administrative Justice

MEMORANDUM FORM

FROM: Ref:

TO:
                                         Date:

SUBJECT:

CHAPTER SIX

TABULATION

Tabulation is broadly distinguished into tables and columnar matter. The information in tables are categorized with the use of horizontal and vertical lines, whereas information in columnar form are categorized only with horizontal headings.

TABLES

Students normally face some difficulties typing tables on a manual typewriter. Unlike on an Electronic Typewriter, which has an automatic framing function, or the Word Processor, which have the Automatic Tables function. Typing tables on a Manual Typewriter involves very careful calculations, and the following procedures may be followed:

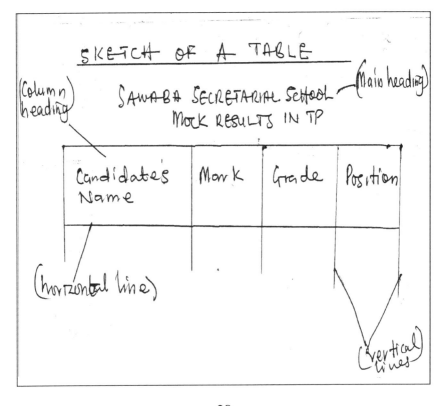

STEP ONE

1. Insert your paper into the typewriter, and straighten it well into the paper guide.

2. Carefully count the number of lines in the original text, and subtract it from the total number of line spaces available on your paper. Then, divide the answer by two and your answer is what you are giving for the Top Margin.

3. Count the longest line under each column heading, and add up the numbers of the available columns in the table

i. Add 3 character spaces to the total number of spaces, separating each column heading, so that when you are ruling the vertical lines, each column will be separated from the vertical lines by one character space

i   Subtract the total from the Pitch or total number of character spaces available on your paper. Divide the answer by 2 and that is for you to set the left and right margins

i. Verify the accuracy of your calculations, by using the space bar to count the number of character spaces apportioned for the matter.

2. From the total number of character spaces in all column headings, including the 3 extra character spaces, set your tabulation keys to these points. Begin the task earnestly and carefully

STEP TWO

You can either center the main heading of the table or block it, depending on specifications. Type the main heading according to specifications.

1. Give three lines spaces and rule the first horizontal line using the underscore.

2. Return the carriage, and further add half line space by turning the platen knob upwards once. Now, type the column headings, which can also be centered or blocked

3. After the column headings, return the carriage and reduce the line spacing by half, by turning the platen knob downwards once. Now rule the second horizontal line.

4.   Begin typing the matter in the table in double or one and a half lines spacing, and carefully. Draw the last horizontal line when you return your carriage after the last line has been typed.

5.   Before removing the paper, use a pencil to mark the points, where the vertical lines will be drawn or typed, depending on specifications. You can use pencil or black pen to rule them, or use the underscore key to rule.

6.   Having made the vertical line points, remove the paper from the typewriter, and insert it back landscape, and carefully rule the vertical lines on the pencil marks already made.

COLUMNAR WORK

Every matter in columns will be typed as such, and the same procedure will be used as in tables, except that, no vertical lines are ruled, Normally the column headings are simply underscored, and the main heading is either centered or blocked depending on specifications.

CHAPTER SEVEN

MANUSCRIPTS

A manuscript is any write-up, which describes, analysis and evaluates and or otherwise, of a phenomenon, event, or any other subject matter. There are various types of manuscripts which a student or qualified secretary may be requested to type. Such manuscripts can be extensive, such as books, extended reports and proposals; pamphlets, newsletters and papers, etc. They can also be short, such as extract materials, short reports and proposals, minutes, contractual documents, etc.

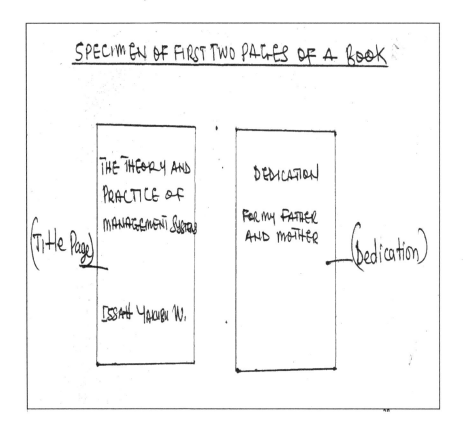

CHAPTER EIGHT

FORMS

Forms are open-ended material designed to obtain specific information about certain individuals, group of people, or entities. The student and secretary will always be required to either type the form or complete the form with the requisite information, or both tasks together. The guidelines for the typing and completion of forms are as follows:

SPECIMEN FORM LETTER

TAMALE POLYTECHNIC

Our Ref: _ _ _ _ _ _ _

Your Ref _ _ _ _ _ _

P. O. Box 3, E/R
Tamale.

Date: _ _ _ _ _ _ _

ADMISSION OF STUDENTS-1994/95 ACADEMIC YEAR

I am pleased to offer you a place on the _ _ _ _ _

_ _ _ _ _ _ _ _ _ _ _ _ _ _ _ _ _ _ _

Programme in the Polytechnic beginning from the date the Polytechnic re-opens on the _ _ _ _ _ _ _ _ _ _

_ _ _ _ _ _ _ _ _ _

_ _ _ _ _ _ _ _   _ _ _ _ _ _ _ _

1. Type all items of the form in double line spacing, unless otherwise specified.

2. It may be centrally displayed on the paper. In which case, careful calculations must be made as in the chapter on tabulation.

3. Give between three to four line spaces, for the signature line.

4. Most importantly, you must understand and decide the correct format for the form before you begin to type it

5. Use the full stop key to type the dotted lines on which information is provided. Type the key lightly, in order not to perforate the paper.

6. When completing the form, give half line space above the dotted line, before typing the information. In other words, ,the information is not typed directly on the dotted lines, since legibility will be hampered.

7. Type the information in capital letters, unless otherwise specified, and very accurately, because information provided on forms can be very special and contentious. Therefore maximum accuracy is necessary

CHAPTER NINE

OTHER DOCUMENTS

The typist may be typing other documents which are not treated in the previous chapters. The typing of these documents depends on your place of work.

MENUS

Menus are list of dishes and drinks available at a particular time in a restaurant or bar. They are typed in different formats: firstly, they can be typed by centering each item on the list on the paper; they can also be typed centering the whole matter in the middle of the paper; thirdly, they can be displayed with the left margin smaller to the right margin.

ITINERARY

Itineraries are typed for Chief Executive Officers or Senior Officers at workplaces, and they contain a list of duty tour schedules. It can be typed on A6, A5, and A4 paper, depending on the length of it.

TABLE OF CONTENTS

Table of Contents are essential parts of manuscripts, providing the guide to the topics and their pages treated in the manuscript. The size of paper used depends on the size of the manuscript.

PROGRAMME

Programmes are a list of activities to be observed on an occasion or event. It can be typed on an A4 , A5 or Quarto size paper, depending on the list of activities..

INVITATION CARDS

Invitations to weddings, funerals, outdoorings, goodwill parties, and others can be beautifully displayed on any paper size, with some beautiful labels and symbols. The features of this document is the ornamentation.

NOTICES

Notices to meetings, and other events, are typed on different paper sizes. Notices to Annual General Meetings of organizations are typed with an agenda.

CHAPTER TEN

SOME IMPORTANT NOTES

ADDRESSING ENVELOPES

Envelopes are foils to letters and other documents meant for postage. Normally, it is the address of the recipient which is typed on the front of the envelope. Sometimes, the sender may wish to type his address on the envelope, so that it can be returned to him, incase it does not get to the recipient. Some other labels can be typed on the envelope, such as: confidential; private; attention; etc. Also, stamps are pasted or stamped on the right corner of the envelope. In order to provide space on the envelope for all these labels, including the recipients address, there is an acceptable positions for all of them.

Position of the Recipients Address

The addressees address can be typed on the envelope at two positions, namely; center position, the address on the envelope is typed such that, the top margin is equal to the bottom margin, and same to the left and right margins; and secondly, positioning it more towards the right margin and more towards the bottom margin, such that, the left and top margins are wider and longer than the other margins respectively.

If you choose to center the recipients address on the envelope, then the addressers address should be typed behind the envelope. On the other hand, if you choose the latter positioning, then the addressers address can be typed on the left hand top corner of the envelope, since ample space is provided.

The other labels can be typed either on the left top corner or middle top part of the envelope.

Furthermore, the addressees address can be typed in three styles: Firstly, it can be blocked; indented;; and each line being centered.

IDENTIFICATION OF CORRECTION SIGNS

Correction signs are corrections made on draft document;   The standard correction signs with alphabetic and symbolic abbreviations are:

ALPHABETICAL
CORRECTION SIGNS AND THEIR MEANINGS

INDTPAR	INDENTED PARAGRAPHS
BLKPARA	BLOCKED PARAGRAPHS
HGGPAR	HANGING PARAGRAPH
ALNMGN	ALIGN OR JUSTIFY MARGINS
SGLE LN	SINGLE LINE SPACING
INTCAPS	INITIALCAPITALS
BLDCHARAC	BOLD, THICKEN OR BLACKEN
BLDHD	BOLD HEADING
DLELN	DOUBLE LINE SPACING
UC	UPPER CASE
US	UNDERSCORE
LC	LOWER CASE
CAPS	CAPITAL LETTERS
SPCAPS	SPACED CAPITALS
SP	SPACE
TRS	TRANSPOSE, OR MAKE CLEARER
D	DELETE
CTR	CENTER
CLSSP	CLOSED SPACED
NP	NEW PARAGRAPH
BLKPARA	BLOCK PARAGRAPH

SYMBOLIC CORRECTIN SIGNS

⭕	BALLOON
✓	CORRECT
⌐	NEW PARAGRAPH
⌐⌐	ALIGN
,.......	STET-TYPE IT
⌐......⌐	RIGHT WORD
◯	INCORECT SPELLING
λ	INSERT
⌣	CLOSE UP SPACE
ⓐ	DELETE AND CLOSE UP SPACE
⌣	RUN ON
⌣	AT
ⓔ	ADD SPACE
⧣	AND
⍺	INSERT
∧	

ABBREVIATION
There are certain standard abbreviations normally found in detailed dictionaries. These kinds of abbreviations can be typed as such in documents, unless otherwise categorically instructed.. Therefore, the kind of abbreviations which poses some difficulty in transcription are those which has to be identified in context. This implies that, the secretary has to be very versed in the English Language, especially grammar and spelling.
The common abbreviations of this nature are:

ABBREVIATIONS AND THEIR MEANINGS

HR	HERE
HV	HAVE
TH	THIS, THESE, THE, THUS
THR	THERE
WH	WHICH
WR	WERE
WHR	WHERE
DIV	DIVISION, DIVIDE
DR	DEAR, DOCTOR
MD	MADAM, MADE
DEV	DEVELOP
DEVT	DEVELOPMENT
DD	DEMAND
SS.	SUPPLY
CHMP	CHAMPION
CHM	CHAIRMAN
CHP	CHAIRPERSON
MNGT	MANAGEMENT
MNG	MANAGE
MGR	MANAGER
ACC	ACCOUNT, ACCOUNTING
ACCT	ACCOUNTANT
SEC	SECRETARY, SECONDARY
SCR	SECRETARY
SCH	SCHOOL
TECH	TECHNICAL

LEADER DOTS

Leader dots are marks of full stops, either in single dots, two or three pairs, that lead the reader from one column item to another in a different column which are related. Leader dots are used in different documents, such as in tables, table of contents, programmes, etc. When you are pairing in two or three pairs, it is recommended you provide equal character spaces in between each pair of leader dots.

DITTO SIGNS

Ditto Signs have no any special character on the keyboard for it, but normally, the comma sign is used to improverise. Otherwise, you may have to manipulate the platen knob to use the quotation marks for it, which is difficult and waste of time.

Ditto signs are used to prevent repetitive typing, particularly material in tables or columns, with one of the items having to be repeated more than once in a row. For example, when you are typing items one to twenty, and the first five items are the same, type only the first item in its full wording, and the next four items use ditto signs for them. This is to save time and energy and prevent fatigue.

CHAPTER ELEVEN

THE COMPUTER

It is important to know the in and out of the place where you are going, and so it is to know the object and structure of the computer, whose use today is very widespread.

DEFINITION OF A COMPUTER
A modern computer is an electronic device which accepts, stores, processes, analyses and produces data for specific purposes, for which it is required to perform.

IMPORTANCE OF A COMPUTER
We study computers for its usefulness in all sphere of life. Man's needs and endeavours have become so numerous, critical and complex that, some of them can no more be handled manually, unless by the sue of electronic devices and sensors, that can perform multiple function.

The world today, as we know is a global village, and the emergence of computer devices, such as the facsimile, telephone, and internet modems are the bedrocks for this development.

Moreover, man's exploits for personal, and business reasons, has given rise to the generation, maintenance and keeping of records. Therefore, the need for a more robust technologies to be applied, has become ever more urgent.

Specifically, man's existence on earth today, is dependant on three complementary spheres, namely, agrarian, industry and service bases. The use of computers in all these areas of man's activities, have gone a long way to improve their accessibility, sustainability and profitability.

Finally but not the least, is the fact that, the comfort and security of our homes and workplaces, calls for the expansion of the use of electronic devices. No piece of work is too voluminous, nor too time consuming now, because, computer have been able to undo the fatigue, frustrations and stress associated with work, both at home and on the job.

TYPES OF COMPUTERS.
Computers can be classified according to their design, time of invention (generation), and general types.
1. Design Types

Under design types, computers can be classified into two broad types; special design and multiple purpose design computers

2.   Due to the generic nature of scientific and technological development, computer development, over the years, have been thought to be the same. The history of the inventions and development of computers are classified under specific generation periods.

i.   First Generation computer: This generation computers, were those invented from the early 1950s to the late 1959. They were the first batch of computers, which used vacuum tubes or valves

ii.   Second Generation Computers: These were computers invented from the later 1957 to the mid 1960s. This generation computers used an improved version of the vacuum tubes or valves technology.

iii.   Third Generation Computers: They were inventions of the period from the mid 1960s up to date. Instead of the vacuum tubes, they used integrated circuits. They were relatively faster and more efficient than the former ones

iv.   Fourth Generation Computers: This generation computers refers to the present day improved versions of computers, which are very enhanced technologically, and have very large-scale memory systems.

More improved Generation computers are envisaged, but until then, there is general consensus that computers will continue to facilitate man's dependence on scientific and technological development.

3. General Technological Typed
Broadly, computers are classified under technology into three:
i.   Digital computers: These types of computers receives, stores and processes data by conversion into discrete numbers of 0,1,3,….. 0. etc.
ii.   Analog computes: They process data in the form of electrical charges, which are usually measured.
iii.   Hybrid computers: This technology combines both digital and analog circuits to operate.

COMPUTER ORGANISATION
A computer is made-up of two main components namely. HARDWARE and SOFTWARE:

1. **Hardware**

   The four major hardware blocks of a multiple purpose design computer are:

i) Memory Unit (MU): This unit is in-charge of the programs embedded in the computer, and all of the data that is computed (inputs) into the computers reside in the memory unit.

ii). Arithmetic and Logic Unit (ALU): This unit receives the data stored in the memory unit for processing. When it processes that data, it either sends back the data to the memory unit, when the user saves it, or sends it to the input and output unit, for production or printing it if the user so wishes.

iii) Input and Output Unit (IOU): This unit performs the linkage between the memory unit and the Arithmetic and Logic Unit. It sends data from the memory unit to the Arithmetic and Logic Unit for processing, and sends back processed data from the Arithmetic and Logic unit to the memory unit for storage. It is also responsible for the output of processed data, by printing out on the printer.

iv) Control Unit (CU): This unit is responsible for the general co-ordination of the various components of the computer. It ensures a harmonious, balanced and systematic role-play within the device. It is the controller, which instructs commands to the other units for optimized output.

2. Software

The software components of the computer are the electronic devices embedded in the computer that allows the device to process and transform data into usable information. For example, in a digital computer the software expresses, processes and transform data in the form of discrete numbers. Another software parts of the computer are the programs packages which routes the various applications of the computer. In addition, the Disk Operation System (DOS) is an important software device in the computer.

The Computer Disk System

The computer uses two main types of disk systems, namely: Floppy Disk or Diskette and Hard disk, which is embedded. However of late computers now have CD drives, where CD ROM and pen devices can be applied.

The Computer Operating System

The computer operating system is about how the computer system operates in relation to the diskette, hard disk, CD pen drives, and other software programs and the information they produce. The most popular computer operating system are Micro soft Disk Operating System (MS DOS) and International Business Machines Disk Operating System (IBM DOS)

DOS is the synonym for Disk Operating System. It manages the computer system to the extent that, without DOS, the software programs cannot work. Therefore, every user of a computer needs to under stand the DOS of the computer.

When you boot or start your computer, the in dictation on your screen, is a display of the DOS prompt (C>) which tells you that you are in drive C, that is, you are operating from the Hard Disk. When you have to use a diskette, then you will change the mode from Drive C> to Drive A>, which is an indication of the floppy Disk in use.

QUESTIONS TO ANSWER (ASSIGNMENTS)
1.   What is a computer
2.   Mention five reasons why we study computer.
3.   Describe the type of generation computers you know.
4.   Mention and describe the basic types of computers we have.
5.   In two paragraphs, describe the historical evolution of computer.
6.   Briefly explain the following terms:
     a   Hardware
     b.   Software
     c.   Input
     d.   Storage
     e.   Output
     f.   Control
7.   What is a printer?

8.   What is the difference between a Hard Disk and a magnetic diskette?

9.   What is the full meaning of DOS? Briefly explain how DOS works and some of its importance.

10. Write the following abbreviations in full:
     a.   MU
     b.   ALU
     c.   IOU
     d.   CU
     e.   DOS

QUESTIONS TO ANSWER - PRACTICALS (TEST)
STEP A

1. Boot the PC
2. Select a program
3. Exit from the program

STEP B
1. Click startup
2. Select new office document
3. Select blank document
4. Type a text

STEP C
1. Click startup
2. Select document
3. Select your file
4. Edit the file
5. Print it
6. Delete it

TASK TO PERFORM (CLASS EXERCISE)
1. Boot your computer
2. Click Startup
3. Explore each of the packages on the menu

QUESTIONS TO ANSWER DURING THE FINAL EXAMINATION IN INTRODUCTION TO COMPUTER

PART ONE - THEORY

CHOOSE ANY 3 QUESTIONS AND ANSWER
1. What is a modern computer?
2. Describe the hardware components of a computer.
3. What do you understand by computer software?
4. Briefly explain any five of the following:
    a. Generation computers
    b. Digital computers
    c. Input
    d. Output
    e. Printer

5. What is the difference between a Hard Disk and a magnetic diskette?
6. What is the full meaning of DOS? Briefly explain how DOS works and some of its importance.

PART TWO PRACTICAL
COMPULSORY QUESTION
1. Process the following commands:
   a. Boot your computer and select Startup
   b. Select new office document / Select Program
   c. Select blank document / Select Microsoft Excel
   d. Type a text of about three paragraphs
   e. Save it and open a file name for it.
   f. Edit it
   g. Print it.

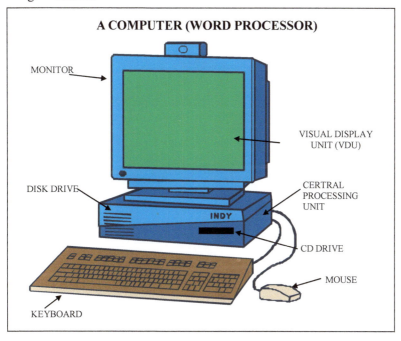

A COMPUTER (WORD PROCESSOR)

MONITOR

VISUAL DISPLAY UNIT (VDU)

DISK DRIVE

CERTRAL PROCESSING UNIT

CD DRIVE

MOUSE

KEYBOARD

CHAPTER TWELVE

USING THE COMPUTER AS A WORD PROCESSOR

It will be very difficult for anyone to use a computer without candidly knowing how to compute the data on the keyboard. Otherwise, you should be ready to spend hours computing the data, which may have taken just some few minutes.

The arrangement system of the keys, and the issuance of commands using the command keys and mouse, are an essential part of using a computer. Therefore, it is always important even for executives who carry with them very portable laptop computers, since the keyboarding are similar.

Another essential aspect of computing, is the fact that, over time, different applications software have come and gone. Nevertheless, all these programs have come without necessarily changing certain features, which remain the same in all the applications. Thus, knowing or even mastering these features will help you a great deal at your workstation, though not necessarily guaranteeing you not to learn the programs

FEATURES ON THE COMPUTER SEREEN (DESKTOP)
The common features on the desktop after selecting a program document are as follows:

1. Windows
This is a rectangular shaped object which can display text or graphical images. When the mouse is used to click this feature, an additional dimension is invoked by the user for interaction with the computer.

2. Title Bar
This feature displays the program running on the computer, and the file name the user is working on.

3. Menu Bar
It displays the functional menu available on the program.

4. Icons:
These are graphical images which serve as short cuts to the menu bar.

FUNCTIONS OF THE MENU BAR
1. File
It is the first feature on the menu bar, and its sub-features are as follows.

a. New: This allows you to open a new document which you wish to process.
b. Open: This allows you to retrieve or access an old document you are already processing
c. Close: It allows you to exit from the document.
d. Save As: It saves a new document, which is not on the computer but you may wish to save.
e. Page Setup: Literally, this feature displays the margin marks on your document.
f. Print Preview: This displays the outlook of the document you are about to print.
g. Print: This function prints the document.
h. Send To: If you click this function, it sends you to a different program you wish to access.
i. Properties: When you activate this function, a dialog box is opened, for you to determine the characteristics of your document.

2. Edit
This edit feature allows you to edit the document you are processing. The following functions are on its sub-menu:

a. Undo - Typing This allows you to delete what you have typed or computed.
b. Redo Auto Correct: This feature brings back or redisplays what you have previously deleted.
c. Cut: This feature allows you to move some part of your document to another part of the same document or different one.
d. Clear and Delete: These features allows you to delete some part or the whole document you are processing.
e. Find and Replace: They allow you to locate the words you wish to change in the document.
f. Copy: This function copies some parts or the entire document to a different portion of the same document or to a different outlet.

3.   VIEW:
This feature provides the user the functions that will allow modifications to the layout of the document. These are:
a. Header and Footer: This allows you to delete the page numbers and replace them
b. Normal: It will allow you to view the document in the normal preview.
c. Full Screen: This will display the document in a full screen size
d. Zoom: This is an expanded view display.

4. INSERT
This feature allows you to insert in your document rows, columns, charts pictures and maps.

5. FORMAT:
This feature allows you to reshape or format the rows and columns you have created in your document.

6. TABLE
This feature will enable you draw or insert tables in your document, based on your specifications of the number of rows and columns.

7. TOOLS
This feature displays a submenu of functions, which includes.
a. Spelling and Grammar: This function is used to verify correct spelling of words and proper grammar structures
b. Word count: This feature will display the number of words the document consist of.
c. Envelopes and Labels: This feature is also available for addressing envelopes and putting labels as designs.

GENERAL GUIDELINES TO ACCESSING A WORD PROCESSING OR SPREED SHEET PROGRAM

STEP ONE (1)
1. Boot the computer
2. Click on startup to display the startup menu.
3. Select your program of choice e.g. Microsoft word
4. Click or enter to display the program document.

STEP TWO (2)
1. Start typing or computing the document.
2. Press control key + S or click the File feature from the menu bar, and select save as.
3. Enter the file name in the dialog box, and click on save or enter to save.
4. Continue computing your document, and make sure at every reasonable intervals, you press the control key + S to save.

SOME IMPORTANT TERMS IN COMPUTER TERMINOLOGY

1. INPUT It is a set of data typed into the computer for processing.
2. OUTPUT It is a set of processed data or information printed out from the computer

3. VISUAL DISPLAY UNIT: It is the computer screen where images and pictures are shown.
4. KEYBOARD: It is similar to the Qwerty typewriter, but with additional functional keys.
5. CURSOR: It is a vertical symbol shown on the desktop, indicating the character space
6. MOUSE: It is a toad-like device used to issue commands as an alternative and complement to the keyboard.
7. PRINTER: A printer is an electronic device used to print out processed data.
8. BOOT: It is the term for starting a computer
9. DOCUMENT: It is the data or information you are working on in the computer
10. DELETE: It is the term for erasing something
11. BLOCK: When you highlight a document in black before effecting a command for its processing.
12. EDIT: When modifying a document
13. SEARCH: It is an attempt to retrieve a document
14. FILE: It is a saved document which is given a name.
15. FOLDER: It contains several files.
16. FONT: It is the size of the characters or typefaces.
17. COMMAND: It is a set of instructions to the computer.
18. HELP: The computer software always offers guidelines when the user faces difficulties.
19. PASSWORD: It is a secret number or letters or a abomination of both to safeguard your combination.